Do you want to
Then this book
– keeps it real!
friend to be tr
demonstrates th

God we find the true object of human curiosity,
comfort, community and beauty.

Natalie Brand
Bible teacher and author of 'Priscilla,
Where Are You? A Call to Joyful Theology'

In a world where pornography is available
freely and anonymously—even carried in your
pocket—teens are consuming porn more than
ever. This resource is a timely, gracious word
for teenage women to engage on the topic
of purity. Helen Thorne-Allenson uniquely
addresses the heart behind why we turn to
pornography, and gives a grander vision for
turning to God, in community, with our hearts'
desires. This book is gospel-saturated, with
encouraging Scriptures to chew on, and it is
also practical, with useful tools and questions
for reflection. I will utilize this resource in
my counseling room, with teenagers as well
as adults.

Hayley Satrom
Counselor and co-host, *Counselling Talks*

There can be few tougher writing tasks than this: to write a book on pornography for teenage girls. Yet I am thankful that Helen has succeeded in writing a book full of wisdom, gentleness, and insight. The deceit of pornography is explained, the promises of Christ held out. There's no pointing fingers, rather this book is oozing with grace, hope and love.

This book would be ideal to use in a 1:1 setting or with a small group of girls. The teaching aim of each chapter is clearly stated and there's helpful reflection questions. Thank you Helen for using your gifts and insights to help those of us who walk alongside our precious teenagers.

Amanda Lansdowne
Youth and Children's Worker,
Redeemer Winchester

TRACK
CHRISTIAN
LIFE

**HELEN
THORNE-ALLENSON**

SERIES EDITED BY
JOHN PERRITT

A (FEMALE) STUDENT'S GUIDE TO
PURITY IN A PORN
SATURATED CULTURE

CHRISTIAN
FOCUS

rym

Copyright © Helen Thorne-Allenson 2024

paperback ISBN 978-1-5271-1171-4

ebook ISBN 978-1-5271-1205-6

10 9 8 7 6 5 4 3 2 1

First published in 2024
by
Christian Focus Publications Ltd,
Geanies House, Fearn,
Ross-shire, IV20 1TW, Great Britain
www.christianfocus.com

with

Reformed Youth Ministries,
1445 Rio Road East Suite 201D
Charlottesville, Virginia, 22911

Cover by MOOSE77

Printed and bound by Gutenberg, Malta

CONTENTS

Series Introduction

Christianity is a religion of words, because our God is a God of words. He created through words, calls Himself the Living Word, and wrote a book (filled with words) to communicate to His children. In light of this, pastors and parents should take great efforts to train the next generation to be readers. *Track* is a series designed to do exactly that.

Written for students, the *Track* series addresses a host of topics in three primary areas: Doctrine, Culture, and the Christian Life. *Track's* booklets are theologically rich, yet accessible. They seek to engage and challenge the student without dumbing things down.

One definition of a track reads: *a way that has been formed by someone else's footsteps*. The goal of the *Track* series is to point us to that 'someone else'—Jesus Christ. The One who forged a track to guide His followers. While we cannot follow this track perfectly, by His grace and Spirit He calls us to strive to stay on the path. It is our prayer that this series of books would help guide Christ's Church until He returns.

In His service,

John Perritt
RYM's Director of Resources
Series Editor

Introduction

Starting to read a book on pornography can bring a whole host of emotions. What are the pages that follow going to contain?

As you start this book, maybe you are:

- Intrigued – keen to find out more about a topic that your friends are talking about, conscious that you do not know much.
- Worried – suspecting that you will be told that what you have been doing is wrong? Aware that you have been watching things that have not been wise.
- Exasperated – fed up with adults talking about a subject that you feel you either know quite a lot about already – or a subject that you do not really want to know about – and here you are with yet another book to read!

- Confused – you have never had any contact with pornography, nor have your friends, but you have been given this resource and you are not sure why?
- Excited – aware that there are good things to learn about God, His world, and yourself, as well as there being lots of ways you can be equipped to help your friends.

Each of us will be in a different place as we begin to read but we all have two things in common: we live in a world where pornography is easy to access at the click of a button and we live in a world where Jesus is King. Working out how to live in such a world, in ways that honor our King, is something we all need to wrestle with day by day.

In the pages that follow, there is going to be no graphic detail about the contents of porn. There will be no manipulating you to feel guilty for decisions you may have made in the past. And there will be no pretending that living for Jesus is always easy. There will, however, be an honest look at who we are, what pornography is, why we are here, and how God is calling us to live – and an invitation to follow Him into a future that is beautiful beyond compare.

SECTION 1: UNDERSTANDING PORN

1. Purpose

———

Have you ever wondered what your purpose is in life? Ever sat down to think about why you are here? Maybe you are aware that God has "prepared good works" for you to do (Eph. 2:10). Maybe you are keen to be involved in missions. Maybe you just want to follow your dreams, use your gifts, and have good relationships with those around you.

None of those things are unusual. But there is more. God calls all of us to be His precious children – to have a relationship with Him – to know that He is our good Father and that we are safe in His family. He cares about the specific things we might do – but He cares even more about who we are and the connection we have with Him.

We are designed to be in a flourishing relationship with the universe's King.

WHO WE ARE

To be a child of God is an astonishing privilege. It is worth taking a moment to let that sink in. To paraphrase Ephesians 1:3-14, to be in God's family means that God has been thinking about us since before the beginning of time. It means that He has called us by name to join Him. He wants us in His family – He is not stuck with us but actively sought us out. He has given us His Spirit to live within us, a seal to keep us spiritually safe forever. And He has surrounded us with other believers in His chosen community, the church.

None of that is because we have impressed Him by our words or our ways – we have not earned His welcome – it is simply an outworking of His love. He is a generous God who moves towards messy people, whose hearts go astray, and does what is necessary to bring them back to Him. His love is so deep that Jesus was willing to leave the glories of heaven to die a hideous death, and rise to a victorious life, just so people like us can be in His family. He has done everything necessary to make us clean, to make us His.

How wonderful to think those things apply to us! (Or they could, if we have not already turned to Him.) Those truths are the reason the Apostle John in his first letter could confidently exclaim,

"See what kind of love the Father has given to us, that we should be called children of God; and so we are" (1 John 3:1 ESV).

Our purpose is to be God's child – to be loved by Him and to love Him in return.

HOW WE LIVE

Our status as children of God changes everything. Being a Christian is meant to be more than going through the motions of attending church, saying some prayers and reading God's Word. Being a child of the King of all things brings with it a royal call: to love God so much that we desire to be like Him. Not just to keep some set of rules that He writes down, not just to look respectable on the outside so we can fit in at church but, deep within, to choose to live lives that are astonishingly beautiful.

The Bible is packed with examples. Romans 12 is one place to turn. There it encourages us to be joyful, persevering, hospitable, loving, forgiving, eager to overcome evil by being extraordinarily kind and good. To use our gifts, to value differences among God's family, to live in countercultural ways. None of that is because we have to. It is all about being so overwhelmed by God's immeasurable grace and love that we choose to respond by living in new ways.

Philippians 2:15 puts it like this. We are to live in Christlike ways:

So that you may become blameless and pure, "children of God without fault in a warped and crooked generation." Then you will shine among them like stars in the sky.

It is about being incredibly beautiful in a world that can be pretty ugly sometimes. And doing so, not in our own strength or in isolation from others – but in God's strength, alongside other Christians who choose to respond to God's mercy and care in that way.

Doing this is a lifetime's pursuit. Day by day, we choose to worship God by living in ways that please Him and are good for us. Year after year, we choose to have our minds renewed by God's Word, so we increasingly see the good in what He wants. Maybe the best word to describe such a life is holy – a life that is set apart to be wholeheartedly and wonderfully centered on Christ.

One aspect of this kind of life is the important matter of how we use our body and mind. Our call is not to go with the flow of the world but pursue something harder, and something far more worthwhile. We are invited to live lives of profound love. Not cheap love – which sees us treating ourselves and others as objects of pleasure – but deep love that knows the true value of both us and those around.

And that brings us to the main topic of this book.

WHAT'S OUT THERE

God's call is the very opposite of pornography's call. Pornography, which at its core is simply media that portrays explicit sexual material, designed to stimulate sexual excitement, is the epitome of cheap love. It tempts people like us to switch on our devices and use our body and mind to get a quick hit of sexual excitement, devoid of any real human interaction or care.

It can feel appealing at times, lots of people can attest to that. It is certainly easy to access and it comes in many forms. In this book we will be focusing on the pornography it is possible to find in video form online – material that can be watched. But there is also plenty of explicit content in books, fan fiction, photography, games, and AI. It's out there but it never offers real love, only fake love. And it always drags us away from God's countercultural call. Using it does not help us shine like stars, it mutes us, dulls and denies our true purpose and call.

WHERE WE'RE AT

Do Christian women and girls actually watch pornography? Is anyone who is reading this book likely to be trapped by its lure? Before we go any further in this book, it is worth clearing up a couple of misconceptions. Frequently I hear two statements and they are both wrong!

Some Christians tell me, "People in churches don't watch porn – and certainly not girls." That is not true. It is estimated that nearly two-thirds of girls will see pornography before the age of eighteen. That is not a small number. Not all those girls went looking for it – about a quarter will have innocently clicked on a link and accidentally opened up some explicit material – but the images will have been seen. And they will not be easily forgotten.

Other Christians tell me, "Everyone watches porn – it's inevitable so just go with the flow." That is not true either. If about two-thirds of girls watch pornography before they are eighteen, that means one third do not. A third of all girls is a lot of girls! It is not weird or unusual to get through your teenage years without seeing explicit content online.

If you have watched pornography – or if you have not watched pornography – you are not alone. You are, however, called to a life full of purpose, a life of fullness in a world where there is pornography all around. A life which is good, kind, loving, beautiful, generous, countercultural, extraordinary, honoring to God and centered on Christ. And what a wonderful purpose that is!

MAIN POINT

God is calling you to be beautiful, to live a holy life of deep love in relationship with Him – a life that is the opposite of the cheap love pornography offers.

REFLECTION QUESTIONS

- Have you watched pornography? What were the circumstances? If you have not seen it, are you thinking about watching, or content not to know? Spend a moment talking to the Lord about where you are at. Simply be honest with how things are going right now.
- What do you think about the purpose God has given your life? What excites or challenges you about His call?

2. Value

It is worth exploring what the problem with pornography really is. There are plenty of people in the world who will say it is pretty harmless – they will describe it as just one person quietly sitting in front a screen, enjoying themselves. And, when compared with things like murder and rape, it hardly seems to be something that should cause us to be disturbed.

The trouble is, that there is so much more going on than one person quietly sitting in front of a screen. And so many more emotions engaged than just pure enjoyment. Pornography devalues and it does so in four important ways:

- It devalues us
- It devalues the people on screen
- It devalues the people around us
- It devalues our relationship with God

PORNOGRAPHY AND US

There is no getting away from the fact that we are changed by what we watch. As we consume media, we are molded by it. Sometimes that can be a good thing – there are many wonderful ways in which the media can inform, inspire, encourage us to take action and give us a whole host of wholesome pleasures to bring us joy. Sometimes it is not such a good thing. Sometimes we are bombarded by lies but, because they come at us so frequently, we lose our ability to spot what they are.

Pornography nudges us to believe a whole host of things that are not right.

It encourages us to think that sex and love do not have to go together. That it is fine to experience arousal apart from a relationship of trust and there are no consequences to that.

It encourages us to believe that we have the right to experience sexual pleasure whenever and wherever we want it – arousal on demand rather than sex as part of a mutually committed covenantal bond.

It encourages us to believe that we are at the mercy of our sexual desires – they are not to be thoughtfully assessed but rather given in to. If our body wants something, we should simply say, "yes."

It encourages us to believe that we, as women, are the sexual playthings of others. Whilst there are some forms of pornography where women get a say, most of the material online portrays us an object, designed for the pleasure of men.

Those things are dangerous. They are not good for us. Thankfully, God's story is better. He values us more.

In Genesis 1-2, we see the story of God making humankind. There He describes us as people in His image (Gen. 1:27). We are made to be people with value, made to be people who reflect God in small ways. And that means we are never objects to be used – or animals at the mercy of out-of-control desires – but people, who should know the safety of loving, committed relationships. We are called to be people who can know the joy of sex in the context of marriage – a lifelong commitment where each person is willing to treasure the other, sacrifice for the other, and respect the other.

Pornography tends to nudge us to think we do not matter, we have no control, that it is okay to be used. And that is a tragedy. We deserve better.

PORNOGRAPHY AND THOSE ON SCREEN

Pornography is no walk in the park for those who act the scenes either. There are some people who willingly engage in sexual activity in front of a camera – for some it is a way of making money that they choose – but, for many, coercion and control lie behind their on-screen performances. Some are trapped by addiction, and this feels like the only way to earn the money to feed their habit. Some are forced into this life by intimidating "boyfriends" who exploit the people they claim to love. Some are trafficked from their homes across the world as modern-day slaves, forced to perform against their will. Some videos online are "revenge porn" – videos taken consensually whilst in a relationship but then posted out of spite, with the aim of humiliating, once the relationship ends. Even those who willingly participate will know the physical suffering – sometimes significant injury – that comes with the scenes that are shot. The stories behind the actors on screen, at times, can make our hearts break.

These people too are image-bearers. They are worthy of love, protection and respect. How awful might it be to live with the knowledge that strangers across the globe are gazing on your naked body, gaining pleasure from your pain. Using pornography devalues the lives of those who are coerced into working in the industry. It ignores their choices, their preferences, their plight. The actors deserve better.

PORNOGRAPHY AND THOSE AROUND US

Because pornography offers a glimpse of sexual experience – something we may well not have had in real life – it can be easy to think that what is offered on screen is what sex is really like. It isn't. Pornography is a fiction – a film.

Marriage may feel like a long way off, but for many of us it will be part of our lives one day. It is tragic how many marriages are wrecked by pornography. Men expect women to be aroused by the kinds of things they have seen online. Most of us aren't. Women imagine we have to engage in the kind of positions and experimentation that pornography displays. We don't. Sex is designed to be an intimate expression of deep and lasting love, not a quick hit allowing one person ecstasy and another shock and pain.

Even before marriage, there can sometimes be real pressure to engage in the kind of activity that pornography shows online. When we are aware others have done something, we can sometimes feel that we therefore ought to say "yes" to it too. We can feel as if others might think we are strange if we decline. But a loving relationship rarely looks like a pornography scene. The two things are often miles apart.

We and our current or future partners deserve a relationship that is tender, kind, fun, mutually loving – and safe. Pornography does not fuel that. It fuels the opposite. Our relationships deserve better.

PORNOGRAPHY AND GOD

Most seriously, pornography encourages us to dump God. To say, "my sexual pleasure is more important than Your purposes for my life." It is not that God is trying to be mean when He says to stay away from sexual impurity (Eph. 5:3) – He is encouraging us to do what is best for us and most like Christ. He is calling us to something beautiful. But pornography nudges us to believe that His will and ways do not matter, that He is just being some kind of killjoy, that it makes more sense to have a bit of fun, that there will not be any consequences.

God is God. He's Lord and King. He also cares. He loves us. He wants us to have a good life. Pornography can never offer that. God deserves better too.

It may be that you have already engaged with pornography – a lot of people reading this book will have been in that place. And now, having read this chapter, maybe there are feelings of guilt or shock running through your head. Please know you are still loved. The God of the universe knows, and He cares for you. He is not wanting you to punish yourself or spiral down. He is offering you a better path, a new way of living, that He is keen to walk with you.

MAIN POINT

Pornography may look harmless at a quick glance but it damages us, damages those involved in making it, damages our relationship with others and damages our relationship with God.

REFLECTION QUESTIONS

- What has struck you about the dangers and damage of pornography? Has anything here been new or particularly challenging? In what ways is God's call on our lives better?

- How might you pray for those involved in the sex industry? Can you pray for them now?

SECTION 2: UNDERSTANDING WHY WE USE PORN

3. Curiosity

Why do you think we – or the friends around us – use pornography? Given the way it devalues so much that is precious, it might be tempting to think that it is easy to say "no." But it isn't. Sometimes the appeal of pornography is very strong. Why is that?

Because it half gives us things we want.

It is important to remember it only half gives us things – it never fully gives us what we really want or need – but it gives us something and that encourages some of us to keep coming back for more. In this and the two chapters that follow, we are going to look at some of things pornography claims to provide.

AN EDUCATION?

Being curious about sex is a perfectly normal thing. It is not in any way weird or disturbing to want to know what sex is, how it feels and what it involves.

We will not all get married – we will not all want to be married – but for those who will be married at some point in the future, sex is going to be part of the relationship. More immediately, sex is in the media all the time. It is quite hard to find programs, movies or books that do not refer to it. And it is a frequent topic of conversation in schools, colleges, and youth programs too.

With so much talk about sex it is completely understandable that we might want to know more. We certainly never want to feel like the only one who does not know what it involves. And we absolutely do not want to go back to the bad old days when women were so ignorant of sex that everything was a massive, and painful, shock on their wedding night. However, our knowledge of sex is designed to grow with our age and stage.

Young children do not need to know about sex. They may be interested in "how babies are made" and telling them a little is fine. For their own protection, in this fallen world, they may well need to know that their body is precious and other people should not touch them in certain places. But they do not need to know the details of sexual positions – that would be age inappropriate. Most of us get that for little kids.

As we grow older, we will discover more. But we do not need to discover everything yet. The Bible reminds us that we are called to grow slowly in our sexual awareness. One of the great love stories of the Bible, the Song of Songs, cautions us not to awaken sexual love until the right time.

The trouble is, we live in a world of instant gratification. If we want to know something, we simply jump on the nearest search engine and ask. Most of us have lost that sense of "I'm happy to wait." God encourages us to reclaim it, for our good.

There is a line to walk here. I am not advocating naivety that leaves us vulnerable to abuse. We need to know enough to be able to identify when people are saying things – or encouraging us to engage in things – that are not good. But there is something beautiful about waiting to discover the intimacy of sex until we are with someone who is utterly committed to God, to us, to our wellbeing and to the mutual flourishing of our lives. That is by far the best environment to discover the details of intercourse.

A RELEASE?

How about the pure, physical drive that many of us experience? It is not just that we are curious about sex, we have hormones that actively nudge us to seek sex. Isn't pornography a safe place to put those drives?

Different women and girls have different sex drives. Some of us are not that bothered about physical arousal, others of us can feel an overwhelming desire, especially around ovulation time. (It is worth seeing if there is a monthly rhythm to your desire to watch porn; if there is, that may well be your hormones in action.) There is nothing better or worse about having a higher or lower sex drive, it is just how we are – part of being fearfully and wonderfully made (Ps. 139:14). But what we do with that sex drive matters.

Some people think that pornography will provide a release for their sexual tension. And, for a few short moments, that is exactly how it feels. But the more we engage in sexual activity online, the more we want it. The more we give in to a behavior, the more it begins to trap us. Indeed, in Romans 6 we read that it is possible to become enslaved to impurity – it might feel like freedom, but it relentlessly keeps us coming back for more. That's exactly what online explicit material does. Pornography is more likely to increase our drive, increase our desire to keep watching, than decrease it – it is not so much of a release as an amplification.

AN OPPORTUNITY TO DISCERN?

What if we have big questions about whether we want to get married? Or big questions about our sexuality? Isn't pornography a good place to test out whether we want to have sex at all or discern whether we really do want to have sex with a man?

If big questions such as these are on our mind, they are good to ask. They are good to bring to the Lord. They are good to bring to trusted adults whose words will reflect the grace, love and truth of God's Word. But they are not good to bring to a porn site. There will be no helpful answers there.

As we were reflecting earlier, pornography does not give an accurate representation of what sex with a real, loving partner is like. It distorts. Did you know that the adult industry employs people to keep the actors aroused? Yes, really. The actual things that the actors are doing are often so painful, impractical, implausible, or just plain drawn-out that they cannot stay aroused without some additional help. That is not what real sex is like.

Real sex, in a loving marriage, is designed to be wonderful. It won't always work seamlessly (nothing ever does!) but it is meant to be a delight. For those who choose not to marry, celibacy is designed to be wonderful too. That won't always feel great either (there needs to be significant effort made to ensure that platonic relationships are strong and overflowing with love) but it also is meant to be a delight. Working out those potential paths, with wise and trusted people who care for us deeply is a much healthier route than trying to figure things out online with a bunch of actors who do not even know our names.

MAIN POINT

Desiring an understanding or experience of sex is normal but pornography does not give us a safe place to explore those desires – waiting for a loving husband, and in the meantime, having conversation with wise and gentle adults will help.

REFLECTION QUESTIONS

- What are some of the questions you have about life, sex, and relationships? Who might be a good, safe, godly adult with whom to have those conversations?

- When are you – or your friends – tempted to go online? What do you think about the fact pornography tends to amplify and enslave rather than offer release?

4. Comfort

———

Not all pornography use is primarily about sex. It always involves looking at sex, but sometimes we engage with it for very different reasons.

Genesis 3 reminds us that the world we live in is broken – fallen, is the theological term. That means that our relationships, our environment, our desires are not as they should be. That, in turn, means we often get hurt.

Most of us know that to be true. Most of us have stories to tell of things in our lives that are deeply painful. Some of us will have experienced the horrors of bullying or abuse – others of us the grief of betrayal or abandonment – still others of us will know the relentless pressure of just trying to get through life each and every day. Even in the best of families, and friendship circles, there are hard things that nudge us to weep.

God is not unaware of our struggles. He cares for us deeply. The Bible describes Him as the God of all comfort (2 Cor. 1:3) – the one who loves to comfort us and then enables us to comfort others. The church is designed to be a place where we all receive the Lord's comfort for the things that are hard and then mutually share that comfort with those around. Sometimes, however, we look for comfort in other places – online.

A CHANCE TO RELAX?

Some people watch pornography because they say it helps them switch off. The pressures of life build up and up and the tensions spiral out of control. The sexual arousal pornography brings is one of the few sensations that is stronger than the feelings of pain. It helps them relax, just for a little while.

The trouble is the feeling does not last. Once the clip has ended and the phone flicked back to the latest social media feed, our problems are still there, the pressures are still bearing down but now they feel even bigger because they are also compounded with a sense of disbelief … did we really just watch that stuff online?

God is a big fan of rest. It is not an exaggeration to say that rest is God's very good idea. In the Ten Commandments, He says that each of us should rest every week; it is the pattern that is best for us. He is also keen that we find refuge from the pressures of this fallen world – that is why so many of the Psalms hold out the offer of God being our rock, refuge, fortress, shelter, shield, or wing. This is how Psalm 18:2 describes him:

The LORD is my rock, my fortress and my deliverer; my God is my rock, in whom I take refuge, my shield and the horn of my salvation, my stronghold.

He is so good at comforting us. No surprise then that He wants us to find that rest and refuge in Him, not online. It is not because He is trying to spoil our fun, but because we are safest with Him.

It makes sense. If we want to be really safe and refreshed, where is the best place to run? Into the arms of a sovereign God who adores us, who is ruling the world with justice and kindness, who is committed to us, in an eternal relationship with us and who provides us with other family members with whom to share life? Or, into a fantasy world of people whom we will never meet, never have a relationship with, never love and who will disappear the moment the clip ends? Looked at in the cold light of day, the answer is clear. The hope, the help, the tenderness and care the Lord provides is so much bigger and more constructive than anything porn can bring to bear.

God is the ultimate comfort – the ultimate source of care.

A CHANCE TO ESCAPE?

But God does not give us the option to deny reality, and pornography's offer to do just that is something that can easily ensnare. When life is utterly overwhelming, a lot of us just want to run away. We want to pretend the bad things are not happening – that things really are going to be okay.

A few moments of escape into a wholesome book or game may be no bad thing. God gives us imaginations to enjoy stories, they expand our horizons, open our eyes to whole worlds of possibility. They can be fun. And, once we put the book or game down, we feel refreshed to engage with reality once more. Wholesome escapism for a little while revitalizes us and there is no problem engaging with God and with His world in the hours that follow. Escaping into pornography may distract but it never spurs us on. No one closes their laptop after watching porn and thinks, "Right, I feel so much better now, let's pray and work out how I am going to persevere." Pornography is the kind of escape that tears down, that leaves us unrefreshed, unrenewed, less equipped to persevere, less inclined to turn to the Lord.

If you have watched explicit material recently, you probably know how hard it is to open God's Word and pray in the hours that follow. You may well know that sense of feeling stuck in your problems rather than encouraged to work out a way through. It promises an escape from our problems, but it just leads us deeper into despair.

A CHANCE TO RELATE?

Maybe one of the hardest forms of pain is loneliness. The Bible reminds us that human beings are designed for community, to share lives, and so it feels desperately hard when opportunities to do that – or do that safely – are taken away. When family or friends let us down, when someone we love dies, or when we move to a new area and simply don't know anyone there – we can feel desperately alone.

The offer of pornography is companionship. It whispers in our ears that there is always someone online ready to perform and tell us things we want to hear. When we want to be wanted, it feels like something that can begin to fill our desire. But those people on screen cannot see us. They do not love us. They can never provide us with the tender care we were designed for.

Only God can do that. He is the only one who is there day and night. He is the only one who can always be there. In Psalm 121:3-4, the psalmist reminds us:

He will not let your foot slip—
he who watches over you will not slumber;
indeed, he who watches over Israel
will neither slumber nor sleep.

He is the one who sees our pain and understands our plight. He is there. And He adores us.

We can turn to Him whenever we want, knowing that He loves to hear our voices. We can be sure of His presence – He does not withdraw His Spirit from those He has chosen to be with Him. We do not have to be all shiny and sorted before we pour out our heart to Him – He is willing to listen to our mess! We can read some of the Psalms, we can hear the real, raw, and gritty vocabulary that people like David used when they were betrayed and afraid. We can emulate them, confident that God hears and will act in the ways He knows to the best.

He provides us with people too. Not perfect people, they will mess up sometimes. But, within the congregation or youth ministry, hopefully there are people you can trust – people who will hear your pain and commit themselves to being with you in it. People who will listen, love and help you think about how to live in this fallen world.

In God and His community, there is true comfort for us all.

MAIN POINT

Life can be deeply painful – we will need comfort and help – but not from porn. Pornography drags us down – God and His people spur us on.

REFLECTION QUESTIONS

• What are some of the hard things you are going through right now? Can you pour out your heart to the Lord, confident He wants to hear?

- What are some of the questions you have about the future? What are some good and healthy ways you can equip yourself to persevere?

5. Control

There are moments when life feels out of control. For all of us there are seasons when our schedule, our choices, even the food we eat seem to be defined – at least to an extent – by others. For some of us, there are harder – devastating – seasons when we seem to have no control even over what happens to our body. Maybe we are facing an extended period of ill health, and the treatment is invasive and unpleasant. Maybe we are facing bullying, and we are being punched or slapped alongside cruel words. Maybe we are being subjected to ongoing sexual abuse, or have been sexually assaulted, and feel deep shame at what has been done to us.

As women and girls, we sadly must acknowledge that one of the outworkings of the fall is that hurt like this does happen. It is wrong. It should stop. We can work to bring about change in the culture. But, right now, it is impossible to ignore the fact that many of us have suffered such pain.

When we are hurt in these ways, it is good to get help from someone trustworthy. Silence never takes away the pain or helps other people change. Talking to wise people – seeking protection and justice – are good and godly things to do. But, even when we do get help, there is an ongoing legacy to such experiences. Some of us decide deep within that we are never going to let our bodies be out of control again.

That decision looks different for different people. Some of us get angry and push others away. Some of us withdraw and choose aloneness over the potential for pain. But it is easy for either response to find an expression online.

AN OPPORTUNITY TO HIDE?

When we have been deeply hurt in real life, we might choose to avoid the complexity of future relationships. We might think, "I'll only have a relationship again, if I can guarantee I won't get hurt this time." But, of course, that guarantee never comes. And so, we begin to substitute real relationships with fake ones – either in cyberspace or in our minds.

Rather than hanging out with people in real life, we hang out online. Rather than allowing ourselves to be fully known, we settle for superficial or mock friendships with the faces we see on screen. We might use pornography to fuel fantasies of how we would like things to be – how we wish things could have been. But they only ever keep us alone.

AN OPPORTUNITY FOR REVENGE?

Others of us harbor anger in our heart. Being angry at abuse is not in itself wrong (God is angry at abuse) but how we express it can utterly devastate both us and those around us. We can dream about getting back at people – dominating those who have chosen to cause us pain – taking control and becoming the one who others fear instead of being the one who lives life afraid. There is plenty of fuel online for fantasies like that, but as we engage in them, we see their ugly side.

Indulging in pornography-fueled images of revenge leads us to even greater pain. Our mind becomes flooded with pictures of suffering, our hearts become hardened to the people around us – we can become all-consumed with the desire to put others down. Such thoughts may stay inside our head – they may spill over into our speech and our behavior – but they drag us down either way and dishonor the Lord.

The Bible tells the story of Tamar in 2 Samuel 13. She was raped by her half-brother and then silenced by her family. The initial violation and the following cover-up broke her – she withdrew and lived as a desolate woman. The lack of justice broke the family – they were torn apart by bitterness, anger and subsequent violence. The situation resulted in despair at one end and murder at the other. It is a horror to read.

What a spur that narrative should be to women like us. A spur to helping keep each other safe. A spur to seeking justice when we do get badly hurt. A spur to processing hard experiences wisely and well, before the Lord, so that we do not end up with bitter hearts that perpetuate the legacy of abuse for generations to come.

None of that safety, justice or healthy processing can be found online. All that lurks in pornography sites is an encouragement to regret, a spur to revenge, or a pathway to getting stuck in unhealthy patterns of thinking and acting. Pornography compounds the pain that comes when others have controlled our body. It is in Christ (often accompanied by wise professionals) that we find the strength to look up, speak out, pursue what is right and ultimately move through the pain to a place of freedom, forgiveness, and peace.

* * *

Over the last few chapters, we have begun to glimpse the ways in which pornography offers us things that look appealing but consistently disappoint. We have begun to reflect on why it is tempting but never fulfilling. We have started to see that whether fueled by our desire for experience, comfort, or control, diving into a world of explicit media will only ever leave us in a worse position than when we started.

Understanding this can be a spur to change. But we need more than understanding to truly change.

God offers a path that is so much better. He is the one who was willing to leave the perfection of heaven to come down to earth. He was the one willing to enter into this world – full of our desires – in order to bring true fulfillment. He was the one who was willing to be obedient to death – even death on a cross, as Philippians 2 reminds.

And His death achieved so much.

In Him we are now forgiven for those moments when our hearts and actions have gone astray. There is no condemnation for those who are in Christ (Rom. 8:1). If we have repented of our wayward desires – or our engagement with pornography – we are clean. This is true for all God's family – His work was complete and effective – we are not stained.

In Him, the power of what has been done to us has been broken. We may not forget the suffering and pain, but it does not have to define us anymore (Col. 2:15). He has broken chains that once trapped us and set us free.

In Him, we have a new life – a righteous life – a calling to holiness (Eph. 1:4). And we have the power of the Spirit to make that life possible. The Spirit who raised Jesus from the dead is alive in us – that is some strength!

If that resonates or intrigues you, keep reading and discover more of what it means to be and stay free.

MAIN POINT

In this fallen world, some of us will feel angry about the ways our body has been controlled by others. Anger may be right but what we do with that anger matters. In pornography there is fuel for bitterness and revenge – in Christ and His people there is fuel for recovery and hope.

DISCUSSION QUESTIONS

- Has your body ever been used in ways which have been outside your control? Is there anyone you could tell? Are there people who can help you stay safe?
- How are you responding to past pain? Are there tendencies in your heart that are leading you away from God? What strikes you about Jesus' work on the cross? How do your risen Savior's achievements bring hope for you today?

SECTION 3: PURSUING CHRIST

6. Strategies

If you are still reading, there is a good chance you either want to break free from using pornography, stay free from using pornography or help your friends do that too. Those are beautiful desires! The Lord is pleased with those Christlike aims (yes, even if you messed up earlier today).

There are lots of ways we can continue to turn to the Lord together in this porn-saturated world. But, just for a few moments, we are going to put those on hold and look at some intensely practical things we can all do together to give ourselves a good chance of going forward porn-free.

Is it worth my writing down practical things that are not particularly centered on Jesus? I think so. Because, whilst our greatest need and our greatest help is Him, there can be lots of other things that help along the way. Indeed, in the Bible – in the book of Proverbs – we are encouraged to live wisely, rather than live as fools. And some of the advice we find there is intensely practical.

KEEP A DIARY

Few of us want to watch explicit material all day every day. There are moments when it is appealing and moments when it is not. It is worth keeping a little diary to work out when we are most vulnerable.

When you find yourself tempted to watch pornography, you can note down what day it is, what time it is, what has been happening and how you are feeling. It is useful to note down all four of those things because, after a while, it is going to be helpful to look for trends.

If temptation is hardest on set days of the month, you are alerted to the fact that your hormones are likely to be playing a part.

If temptation is hardest at a particular time of the day – late at night when you are alone, or on the way home from school after a particular lesson – you are alerted to particular times when you may need to find other ways of coping with the stress.

If temptation hits after a certain activity – then you might want to consider whether it is wise or not to continue in that activity (or whether you can engage in that activity in a slightly different way).

If temptation hits in conjunction with specific emotions, like anxiety or fear, then you are alerted to the fact that it is time to find healthier strategies to manage those feelings.

Information helps. Knowing ourselves better equips us to walk wisely and well through times of temptation.

SEEK ACCOUNTABILITY SOFTWARE AND RELATIONSHIPS (AND DON'T TURN THEM OFF!)

There are plenty of free (and not free) accountability programs out there. The best are the ones that don't just block sites or flash up warnings about inappropriate content but the ones that share online habits with a trusted family member or friend. Pornography use thrives in secret corners – if we keep our habits hidden, we have little hope of battling its snare – but building a small and trustworthy community around us can be an immeasurable help. Together we can live a better way.

Maybe as a church youth group you might like to all put the same software on your phones.

Maybe as a family, you could choose to all live above reproach?

When sharing your browsing history with others, it is essential that the person chosen is going to handle that information well. We do not want to share our habits with someone who is going to be angry, legalistic, or gossipy – nor someone that is going to just laugh and think what we are doing is okay – rather someone who is full of love, wisdom, mercy and grace. Someone who can quietly get alongside us when we mess up and say, "Let's talk. I'm here to help. Shall we pray?" Someone with whom we are happy to be open and honest. They may also be people with whom we can just talk about the general hardships of life – people we can message with temptation hits.

Hopefully we all have someone like that in our lives. If not, praying for them to come along may be the next step.

ENGAGE IN MEDIA FASTS

I know it can feel like our phone is an essential life-force but really it is not. Useful for communication, to be sure; handy for emergencies, without doubt; a source of entertainment, it certainly can be; but it is not oxygen, shelter, or food, which means it is something we can go without.

It may be that you do not use your phone very much – if so, praise God that you are living wisely already. But, if, like me, you have a tendency to grab your phone a little too often, it is good to have days or weeks when we leave our media behind. Doing so helps get our view of our phones – and other devices – back into perspective. A media fast is one way to do that.

A media fast does not entail casting our electronics into the local lake! It simply means having them switched off or set to silent for certain hours or days. (Most phones have a setting which enables calls from designated people – like parents – to get through in an emergency, even when all other calls will go straight to voicemail.) As a church group, you might like to nominate days or times when you all do this together, it may feel less weird that way. But deliberately setting aside our technology for a bit will enable us to learn new ways of coping when life feels hard – healthier ways, which will have a positive impact on every aspect of our lives, including our pornography use. It will nudge us to turn to Christ and real-life people who care for us, rather than a screen, when life is tough.

DEFINE DISTRACTION TECHNIQUES

When temptation hits, it is wonderful to read God's Word and pray. There we have such power and hope. However, it can also be handy simply to fill our minds with something wholesome – something that is not porn. The Bible encourages us to think about things that are good:

Finally, brothers and sisters, whatever is true, whatever is noble, whatever is right, whatever is pure, whatever is lovely, whatever is admirable —if anything is excellent or praiseworthy—think about such things. (Phil. 4:8)

Such things can include the beauty of creation, the delight of a favorite band, the love of a particular sport or craft – even the family dog or cat.

Finding something good with which to distract ourselves is not a waste of time. It is about finding new, pleasing, godly, healthy ways of dealing with life. In taking exercise, we are releasing stress, getting some fresh air, providing ourselves with new perspectives and maybe even bringing ourselves into contact with people who can bring us joy. By doing some baking, we are being creative, stimulating our senses in wholesome ways, providing ourselves with pleasure – and maybe blessing others at the same time.

Fighting and fleeing temptation are both biblical calls. The more help we can give ourselves – and others – to do that the better. It is not weakness but wisdom to put practical strategies in place.

MAIN POINT

In order to fight the temptation to use pornography, it is wise to come up with some strategies to help us notice when we are struggling, include other people in our pursuit of holiness and find ways of distracting ourselves.

QUESTIONS FOR REFLECTION

- What accountability do you have in place? What might it be useful to seek?
- What can you do as a distraction technique if and when temptation hits?

7. Hope

Practical strategies are helpful, but they can only go so far. If we are tempted to use pornography, battling habitual pornography use or aware that our friends are finding life hard, it is good to seek the kind of full and lasting heart change that will lead to a life of freedom.

If we are using pornography already, it is worth starting that heart change sooner rather than later. As we may already know, the longer we have been doing something, the harder it is to change. Catch something early and it is so much easier to turn around.

We cannot achieve that kind of heart change by ourselves, though. For that, we need Jesus.

A METHOD OF CHANGE

Thankfully, God does not leave us ignorant of how to change. In His Word, He sets out many models of change. The simplest can be found in Ephesians 4:22-24, where Paul likens the process of heart change to the process of changing our clothes (something we hopefully mastered some time ago!).

He calls us: *to put off your old self, which is being corrupted by its deceitful desires; to be made new in the attitude of your minds; and to put on the new self, created to be like God in true righteousness and holiness.*

Simply put, he acknowledges that we all have things it would be good to stop doing – things it would be good to start doing – and things that we need to understand and believe to make that possible.

This is not designed to be a simplistic model. This is not Paul saying, "stop using pornography – start praying – and in the meantime, read your Bible more." That would be incredibly trite. Rather, it is a nuanced structure in which we bring our struggles to the Lord for gradual transformation – progressive sanctification (to use the theological term).

What does that look like in practice? Often, it is good to start with one of our underlying beliefs. Maybe we use, or are tempted to use, pornography because we feel unloved. First of all, we need to notice that is what we are doing. We need to be alert to the fact that we are feeling that way and catch those thoughts. That might sound odd but, as humans, we are pretty talented at thinking a whole host of things under the radar and not being particularly aware of the damage the things we are saying to ourselves are doing! This process of noticing is what the Bible calls, "taking every thought captive" (2 Cor. 10:5) – it is about being alert to our thought processes and not just letting them slide.

Once we have noticed such a thought, we want to call it what it is: an old-self thought. What does that mean? An old-self thought is a thought that comes easily to us, probably because we have practiced it so much, but one that is at odds with our Christian faith. It is something that has no place in the Christian's mind – because it is not true. So, whenever we find ourselves thinking, "no one loves me," we can catch it, notice it, label it and acknowledge that it is not true.

"But it feels true," you might be thinking. Yes, at times, it does. But that does not make it true. Sometimes our feelings lie to us. God says it's not true. And, given He never lies (see Num. 23:19), it is good to believe Him.

The next step is to give ourselves lots of evidence that we are, indeed, loved. We might do a little bit of that by talking to people who love us. But we do well to do the majority of that by engaging with God's Word. In the Bible, there is overwhelming evidence that He adores us. All of us. He made us, knitted us together in our mother's womb (Ps. 139:14). He provides for us each day, calls us into His family – and, in Jesus, even died for us! Love does not get stronger than that. That probably will not all sink in on day one but as we keep reminding ourselves of how loved we are, our minds begin to transform.

Little by little, whenever we catch ourselves thinking, "no one loves me" we can begin to replace that with, "actually, no, I'm loved – loved with an unbreakable love – and I will be for all eternity." As that happens, we gradually begin to take off our old self and put on our new.

We will want to do that with a whole range of old self beliefs: I'm useless, I'm pathetic, I can't change, etc. And, in Christ, gradually move to the place where we can confidently say, "God has gifted me, I have value and purpose, and I am changing in the power of the Spirit."

We will want to do that with some of our behaviors too. Logging on to view pornography is an old-self behavior, we may want to remind ourselves of that each time we do it, remind ourselves of the call to something better, and little by little, practice running to prayer, God's Word, real life treasured relationships and our distraction techniques in the quest to put on our new.

A LIFE OF CHANGE

I want to be honest, change like this does not happen overnight. It can take us a while to even start noticing our old-self thoughts, even longer to believe what the Bible says is true about God and us. It can be tricky to put on new ways of thinking and acting but it is possible, because God is active. We will need to keep going, in His strength, accepting that change takes time but is good to keep pursuing anyway.

We cannot change everything all at once. No one can. But we can make a start. It is often wise to pick one belief and one behavior and work on those. If you are ensnared in regular pornography use, you might want to pick something like:

- Old-self Belief: I can never change.
- New-self Belief: I can change, in the power of the Spirit
- Old-self Action: I will just turn off my accountability software.
- New-self Action: I will keep the software on and talk to my accountability partner about what is going on.

At all times, it will be important to remember God's promise to us that, "he who began a good work in you will bring it to completion at the day of Jesus Christ" (Phil. 1:6 ESV). God means what He says. We can change and grow. And, as we do, we can celebrate every little victory. Each time we catch a thought, each time we battle temptation, each time we turn back to God after we have messed up, those can all be little moments of joy as we see God working out His promise in us.

THE CONTEXT OF CHANGE
It is also worth saying that the framework set out in Scripture is set in a relational context. It is not just that God wants us to take off old actions, put on new actions and think differently in between, He wants us to do that in the company of others.

Ephesians 1, which comes just before this passage on change, reminds us that God is the God who calls us into community with Him.

In love he predestined us for adoption to sonship through Jesus Christ, in accordance with his pleasure and will – to the praise of his glorious grace, which he has freely given us in the One he loves. (Eph. 1:4-6)

The rest of Ephesians 4, the immediate context for these change verses, speaks clearly of the need for one another. Church isn't just about reading the Bible or listening to preachers, we are designed to grow and mature as we do life together – serve each other – and speak into each other's hearts.

So Christ himself gave the apostles, the prophets, the evangelists, the pastors and teachers, to equip his people for works of service, so that the body of Christ may be built up until we all reach unity in the faith and in the knowledge of the Son of God and become mature, attaining to the whole measure of the fullness of Christ. (Eph. 4:11-13)

Why is that important? Because Ephesians 4:22-24 could all sound a bit like an impersonal change system. Do this – do that – and all will be fine. But it is so much more than that. It's a process of change that is designed to take place when we are surrounded by love, encouragement, role models, grace and hope. We will look at this idea more in the next chapter.

A CHANCE TO CHANGE

What about timing? When is it a good time to start pursuing change? Should we wait until the holidays are over? Pick this process up at new year? Maybe think about it for a while? All options, I suppose.

I am not writing to pressure you into any particular course of action, but I think it is fair to say: today is a really good day to begin that process of change. Maybe a better question might be: why wait?

You do not need to solve everything in one day, you do not need to be sure you can get everything right from here on in, just take a baby step. And, in the power of Christ, explore how this road to freedom is going to go.

MAIN POINT

We can all change. Little by little – in the power of the Spirit and with the help of our friends – we can gradually take off our old self beliefs and behaviors and put on new.

REFLECTION QUESTIONS

- Can you identify one belief and one behavior to put off and put on? What might they be? (Please just pick one at a time not more.)
- How can you encourage yourself to remember that, even when change is not fast, it is still possible?

8. Community

In Chapters 6 and 7, we touched on the need for others to help in this journey. I am going to take a wild guess and assume that at least some of us have decided to skip that bit and try to go it alone.

The instinct for privacy is understandable. It is a basic human response. Ever since the fall in Genesis 3, we have been trying to hide our waywardness from God and others rather than being open with those around us. But there is something ensnaring about keeping things quiet. When we keep our struggles hidden, they somehow seem to amplify, become insurmountable and our strength to battle them seems to ebb away.

Whilst we should never be in a position where we have to tell everybody everything – that would be both hideously embarrassing and deeply unwise – we are all in a position of needing people around us. That is simply the way we were designed to thrive.

What kind of community do we need?

A CHRIST-CENTERED COMMUNITY

There is wisdom in the world. There is absolutely no shame in seeing a non-Christian doctor, reading non-Christian books, talking to wise non-Christian friends and, where necessary, taking prescribed medication or trying some secular relaxation techniques. But God has designed the process of change, so it takes place best in the community of the church. He has done that because that is where we will find other like-minded people who share the same values, are on the same journey, and are united with us by the same Spirit.

It is in the church that we find people who can model holiness for us. It is in the church that we find people who can model repentance, perseverance and hope. It is in the local congregation that we find people who are willing to open Scripture with us, pray with us, encourage us to keep our eyes on Christ. In the words of Hebrews, it is in the community of believers that we engage in the fine art of spurring one another on to love and good works (Heb. 10:24). It is in the church that God is most particularly at work – bringing about His good purposes and making His people ever more like Christ.

Within the church there will be people we talk to a lot and people we talk to a little. There will be people who know a lot about what is going on in our lives and people who know a little. We absolutely do not want to be telling everyone how we are doing – that is not wise. But we are called to be known well enough by some of the church members (our peers and those older than us) so that together we can all fulfill the biblical call to weep with those who weep and rejoice with those who rejoice (Rom. 12:15). If people do not know we are weeping, they cannot weep with us and that makes it impossible for them to help us lament, to bring us comfort and to offer us hope.

A VISIBLE COMMUNITY

Isn't an online support group better if I am really struggling? For those of us who are really in the depths of pornography use, and struggling to break free, it can be really helpful to have some contact with others who are struggling in similar ways. The sense of understanding and acceptance those groups provide can be wonderful. But there are dangers in teens being involved in those forums which are often designed for adults and may discuss very adult things. And there are shortcomings in only being known by others online.

When people know us in real life, they get to casually observe us day by day. They see our gifts, experience our kindness, become alert to our weaknesses and our wayward ways. When online, it is tempting to give a rather more glossy spin on who we really are. We may be tempted to bump up the ways we have been hurt and diminish the ways we have hurt others – we tell stories from our perspectives alone, and that can often be skewed.

It is healthiest to pursue change within the context of people we can actually meet. It is best to live lives in the view of godly people who will keep loving us as we display the good, the bad and the ugly of our lives. Sometimes those will be friends, sometimes those will be parents, youth ministers, pastors or counselors. All have value. All can help us become like Christ amid people who know the real us, not just a façade.

AN AUTHENTIC COMMUNITY

What doesn't help is pursuing change in some kind of fake community. A community where everyone else is pretending to be godly and sorted rather than pursuing their own change.

The best kind of environment for change is one where everyone is honest about their needs with a group of others, everyone is confident in hope in Christ, and everyone is committed to spurring on the people closest to them. This is not about the strong helping the weak but everyone acknowledging that they are weak and in need of both God's help and the help of their friends. After all, God's power is made perfect when we know we are weak. Paul writes this in 2 Corinthians 12:9:

But he said to me, "My grace is sufficient for you, for my power is made perfect in weakness." Therefore I will boast all the more gladly about my weaknesses, so that Christ's power may rest on me.

It is not a case of God helping those who help themselves! God helps those who humble themselves and know their need. A Christlike community, however big or small, is one where it is safe to be weak, safe to acknowledge sin – a community that is quick to offer mercy and practical help, a community that is dripping with grace.

A REPENTING COMMUNITY

In short, the kind of community that encourages us to thrive is the kind of community where people are quick to repent and believe. The kind of community where people can say Psalm 51 together without fear:

Have mercy on me, O God,
according to your steadfast love;
according to your abundant mercy
blot out my transgressions.
Wash me thoroughly from my iniquity,
and cleanse me from my sin! ...

Create in me a clean heart, O God,
and renew a right spirit within me.
Cast me not away from your presence,
and take not your Holy Spirit from me.
Restore to me the joy of your salvation,
and uphold me with a willing spirit.

Then I will teach transgressors your ways,
and sinners will return to you.
Deliver me from bloodguiltiness, O God,
O God of my salvation, and my tongue will
sing aloud of your righteousness.
O Lord, open my lips,
and my mouth will declare your praise. (ESV)

The kind of community where we know we will all mess up, but that it is good to come back to God and where we can be confident He will forgive us. The kind of community that is serious about holiness and serious about loving people well as they develop that holiness together.

Whatever our engagement with pornography, we can all be part of a community like that – seeking what is best for ourselves and those around us, seeking grace, seeking Christ.

MAIN POINT

We need other people as we pursue holiness – we need our local church and the encouragement of those Christians who know the grace and hope of Christ – and they need us.

REFLECTION QUESTIONS

- How can you help your church, or your youth ministry, grow to become ever more this kind of community?
- What does openness look like for you, in your situation?

9. Beauty

It is not too hard to desire a porn-free life while reading a book like this. It is not too hard to talk about the wonder of a porn-free life when chatting to parents, a pastor or youth minister. And, maybe, in our hearts we would like to be able to click our fingers and go into the rest of our lives confident we will never have contact with explicit material again. But, put down this book and return to whatever you were doing before you started to read, and it is possible that temptation may hit. If that is not what it is like for you, it is what it will be like for at least some of your friends.

The simple fact of the matter is, there will be days when it is easier to give in to temptation than pursue Christ. Every step of the way, though, there will be a choice. And it is possible to persevere – especially if we remember four important things.

ONE STEP AT A TIME

The Bible shows that growth in us is like growth in plants – it takes time – fruitfulness is a gradual process.

When we were adopted into God's family, God gave us Jesus' righteousness. From that day, He started to see us through the lens of the cross, He started to describe us as His holy people. But God knows we still struggle. We are holy by status, but we also have to work out our holiness day by day. He knows that, as our Shepherd, He has to lead us one step at a time through this complex thing called life.

Please do not panic if you cannot get it all right today. You have tomorrow, and the next day, and every other day until Jesus returns to work this out. He is calling us all to walk towards Him, one step at a time. A wholeheartedness to live Christ's way is a good thing, but there is no expectation of instantly being able to do everything right.

MESSES CAN BE FORGIVEN

That means, that God is deeply aware that we are going to need to keep tapping into the grace that He offers! And we can do so confident His supply of mercy is not going to run out.

There may be moments when we watch pornography again. Even if we do manage to stay porn-free, there will be some other pit we fall into. That is what it is like to be human. But, just as the prodigal son in Luke 15 was able to run back into his father's arms, so can we.

The son in that parable knew he had messed up badly. He knew he did not deserve forgiveness. But he got it anyway because his father was good. When we are in Christ, our Heavenly Father is just like that.

The son said to him, 'Father, I have sinned against heaven and against you. I am no longer worthy to be called your son.' But the father said to his servants, 'Quick! Bring the best robe and put it on him. Put a ring on his finger and sandals on his feet. Bring the fattened calf and kill it. Let us feast and celebrate. For this son of mine was dead and is alive again! He was lost and is found!' So they began to celebrate. (Luke 15:21-24)

Each time we mess up, we can fight the temptation to sit in the pigsty of the consequences that our actions have brought about. We can shun the lies that whisper, "God doesn't want anything to do with you now." We can turn our gaze back to Him, say we are sorry, ask for His forgiveness, commit to living under His Lordship once more and know, without any shadow of doubt, that He will welcome us home. Not just a begrudging, "I suppose I can give you once more chance" but an overwhelming joyful sense of "I am so glad you are home."

God loves when we repent and come back to Him. We can love repentance – live repentance too – no matter how many times it takes.

BEAUTY IS ON THE HORIZON

And we can do all of that, confident that perfection is ahead. We may have moments when we get muddled in the here and now. We may have seasons when our stubborn hard hearts seem to hold sway. But His grip on us will not falter or fail. He does not lose His children. And there will be a day when neither we – nor our friends – will struggle with pornography ever again.

In the new heavens and the new earth, there will be no more pain, no more temptation, no more sin. We will be there, alongside our brothers and sisters in Christ, worshiping around the throne of the King – praising Him for eternity – confident that our battles are a thing of the past. The Shepherd leads us to His victory feast (Ps. 23:5-6)

He has made us – made you – beautiful now. But what we are is just a pale reflection of what we will one day become. It is worth holding on for that day.

HE IS WORTH IT

In the meantime, as we face the ups and downs of life, as we battle the temptation of pornography use, as our minds are constantly bombarded with the world's mantra that we can do whatever we want, be whatever we want, and there should be no consequences … we can know that He is worth it. He is worth our all.

God warns us that the Christian life involves picking up our cross and following Christ (Mark 8:34). He is realistic that there will be moments when the world thinks we are mad. But He also offers us the opportunities to lay our burdens on Him. His invites us:

Come to Me, all you who are weary and burdened, and I will give you rest. Take My yoke upon you and learn from Me; for I am gentle and humble in heart, and you will find rest for your souls. For My yoke is easy and My burden is light." (Matthew 11:28-30)

He gives us the chance to labor in His strength, not our own. And He guarantees that the relationship we have with Him will be so special, so close, so loving, so kind, so transformational – so eternal – that the battles will be absolutely worth it, each and every day.

Remembering those four things will help us to keep going, to keep living for Jesus – to keep flourishing, even when it is hard. They will enable us to keep persevering, even when we have messed up yet again. And little by little we will grow, we will change and, in the kindness of the Lord, can reach a place where we live pornography-free for the rest of our lives. Where we can live in ways that are increasingly lovely, pure, Christlike, kind, and beautiful – ever closer to what Jesus designed us to be.

MAIN POINT

Change does not happen overnight, we need to keep going. We do that best, one step at a time, living a life of repentance and faith, knowing that perfection is ahead and Jesus is worthy of our all.

REFLECTION QUESTIONS

- How might your future be different, better, if you choose to follow Jesus in this area of your life?
- What are your next steps going to be?

Appendix A: Next Steps

My writing is almost done. Your reading is coming to a close. There is more that could be said. There are many other things that are going to fill the rest of our days. But let me end with three final things:

YOUR DECISION

I cannot make you act on the content of this book. I do not intend to try. Your walk with the Lord is your responsibility and only you can decide what comes next. I hope you will shun pornography – I hope you will pursue Christ, who is better by far – but your next step is to decide what you are going to do with your body and mind. So, let me ask you: what will you choose today?

MY PRAYER

I will pray for you. And my prayer is this: that you would know God's comfort for the things that pain you; freedom from the things that ensnare; hope for the life ahead of you and strength to follow Christ's ways. I pray that you will see the wonder of Jesus and know that you are safe in His arms. I pray that you will have the courage to repent and believe on those days when it all goes horribly wrong. I pray that pornography will not feature in your future, but that beauty and holiness will flourish in its place.

GOD'S PROMISE

The words that matter most are Christ's, not mine. So let us give the final words to Him. He is offering you wonder and freedom. Go for it. What a future He defines ... As we engage with Him, we can become more like Him. And doing so is beautiful beyond compare.

And we all, with unveiled face, beholding the glory of the Lord, are being transformed into the same image from one degree of glory to another. For this comes from the Lord who is the Spirit. (2 Cor. 3:18 ESV)

Amen.

Appendix B: Further Resources

If you are wanting help to live for Christ and battle pornography, please speak to a trusted adult in your biological family or church family. They should be able to guide you wisely and well.

If you want to read some more, why not try one of these books:

Purity is Possible by Helen Thorne (The Good Book Company, 2014).

Or another book in the Track series:

A Student's Guide to Anxiety by Edward Welch (Christian Focus, 2020).

A Student's Guide to Womanhood by Abigail Dodds (Christian Focus, 2022).

A Student's Guide to Social Media by Jason Thacker (Christian Focus, 2023).

Or see if your youth minister would like to help your group work through this:

Real Change for Students by Andrew Nicholls and Helen Thorne (New Growth Press, 2019).

Live beautiful and free!

Reformed Youth Ministries (RYM) exists to serve the Church in reaching and equipping youth for Christ. Passing on the faith to the next generation has been RYM's mission since it began. In 1972, three youth workers who shared a passion for biblical teaching to high school students surveyed the landscape of youth ministry conferences. What they found was a primary emphasis on fun and games, not God's Word. They launched a conference that focused on the preaching and teaching of God's Word – RYM. Over the last five decades RYM has grown from a single summer conference into three areas of ministry: conferences, training, and resources.

- **Conferences:** RYM hosts multiple summer conferences for local church groups in a variety of locations across the United States. Conferences are for either middle school or high school students and their leaders.
- **Training:** RYM launched an annual Youth Leader Training (YLT) event in 2008. YLT is

for anyone serving with youth in the local church. YLT has grown steadily through the years and is now offered in multiple locations. RYM also offers a Church Internship Program in partnering local churches, youth leader coaching and youth ministry consulting services.

- **Resources:** RYM offers a growing array of resources for leaders, parents, and students. Several Bible studies are available as free downloads (new titles regularly added). RYM hosts multiple podcasts available on numerous platforms: The Local Youth Worker, Parenting Today, and The RYM Student Podcast. To access free downloads, for podcast information, and access to many additional ministry tools visit us on the web – rym.org.

RYM is a 501(c)(3) non-profit organization. Our mission is made possible through the generous support of individuals, churches, foundations and businesses that share our mission to serve the Church in reaching and equipping youth for Christ. If you would like to partner with RYM in reaching and equipping the next generation for Christ please visit rym.org/donate.

Christian Focus Publications

Our mission statement —

STAYING FAITHFUL

In dependence upon God we seek to impact the world through literature faithful to His infallible Word, the Bible. Our aim is to ensure that the Lord Jesus Christ is presented as the only hope to obtain forgiveness of sin, live a useful life and look forward to heaven with Him.

Our books are published in four imprints:

CHRISTIAN FOCUS

Popular works including biographies, commentaries, basic doctrine and Christian living.

CHRISTIAN HERITAGE

Books representing some of the best material from the rich heritage of the church.

MENTOR

Books written at a level suitable for Bible College and seminary students, pastors, and other serious readers. The imprint includes commentaries, doctrinal studies, examination of current issues and church history.

CF4•K

Children's books for quality Bible teaching and for all age groups: Sunday school curriculum, puzzle and activity books; personal and family devotional titles, biographies and inspirational stories — because you are never too young to know Jesus!

Christian Focus Publications Ltd,
Geanies House, Fearn, Ross-shire,
IV20 1TW, Scotland, United Kingdom.
www.christianfocus.com
blog.christianfocus.com